THE JAPANESE CRANE

THE JAPANESE CRANE

Bird of Happiness

Dorothy Britton / Tsuneo Hayashida

Foreword by S. Dillon Ripley

KODANSHA INTERNATIONAL
TOKYO, NEW YORK, & SAN FRANCISCO

The publisher would like to thank the following temples and institutions for allowing reproduction of objects in their collections: Kobe Municipal Archaeological Hall, 6; Kyoto National Museum, 58; Rakuto Iho-kan, 71; Tofuku-ji Reiun-in, 61; and Tokyo National Museum, 67. Thanks are also due the following for their assistance: Dr. Carmen Blacker, Heibonsha Ltd., Dr. Hiroyuki Masatomi, Ken Takahashi, and Masashi Yoshii. The quotations from *Thousand Cranes* by Yasunari Kawabata are from Edward Seidensticker's translation of the work.

PHOTO CREDITS: Eisei Bunko Foundation, 60; Heibonsha Ltd., 67; Keizo Kaneko, 68; Mainichi Shinbunsha, 58; MOA Museum of Art, 64; Suntory Art Gallery, 59; and Tokyo National Museum, 62, 65, 66, 71.
Maps by Michio Kojima. Line drawings by Kazuko Katakura, Yoshito Suzuki, and Tomoko Miyashita.

Distributed in the United States by Kodansha International /USA Ltd. through Harper & Row, Publishers, Inc., 10 East 53rd Street, New York, New York 10022. Published by Kodansha International Ltd., 12–21 Otowa 2-chome, Bunkyo-ku, Tokyo 112 and Kodansha International/USA Ltd., 10 East 53rd Street, New York, New York 10022 and 44 Montgomery Street, San Francisco, California 94104. Copyright © 1981 by Kodansha International Ltd. All rights reserved. Printed in Japan.
First edition, 1981   ISBN 4-7700-0970-4

Library of Congress Cataloging in Publication Data

Britton, D. Guyver (Dorothy Guyver), 1922–
    The Japanese Crane: Bird of Happiness.

    Bibliography: p.
    1. Japanese Crane. 2. Birds in art. 3. Birds in
    literature. I. Hayashida, Tsuneo. II. Title.
    QL696.G84B74   598'.31   81–82027
    ISBN 0–87011–484–0   AACR2

FOREWORD

It was a misty morning in June, 1960, when we drove out from Kushiro toward the great marsh, the nesting ground of the Japanese Crane, on the northern island of Hokkaido. Fog lay over the land, and once away from the city noise, all was quiet except for the grating notes of reed warblers and the twitter of buntings in the sedge. The road was bounded near the marsh itself by a series of towers carrying high-tension wires, with the occasional stump of an old telephone pole or the skeleton of a tree. We could not see the marsh clearly for the mist. Only here and there, parting skeins showed the remains of last year's reeds, brown stalks among the new grass growing in the marsh water.

Snipe drummed, flying down in zigzags, sometimes to land and whistle from a pole perched high above the water. We stepped out onto the embankment road and waited for the mist to rise, hoping to see what we had come for, the great white and black shapes of cranes. Suddenly at a distance we heard a series of resonant calls, an unmistakable throaty trumpeting. How many of them were ·there, and where? We turned away from the marsh's edge and looked out over the fields bordering the road. There they were, five broad-winged silhouettes flying down toward the marsh behind us. And then a strange and breathtaking thing happened. As they began a gliding descent, straight through the high-tension wires between the suspending towers, one crane suddenly described a parabola in flight. A wing tip had clipped a single wire, whirling the entire bird off balance in a tight circle up into the air. Miraculously it righted itself, shuddered, shaking its wing feathers, and resumed its slow majestic descent toward the four shapes now heading down below it. The mist had cleared enough for us to see the five birds, on course, all land safely in fields of budding vegetation a quarter of a mile away. There they proceeded to ruffle their wings, dance a step or two, and quietly settle down to feed.

We turned to our friend Dr. Yamashina, breathing again, realizing how tense the last few moments had been, and how strange it was that one of less than two hundred cranes then in Japan had just escaped electrocution, without even breaking a wing.

Dr. Yamashina, Japan's foremost ornithologist, head of the nation's main bird protection society and the Yamashina Institute in Tokyo, smiled. "Yes, that was a piece of luck," he said.

Two years earlier, in the wake of a program enhanced by radio and newspaper publicity and led by the Yamashina Institute and the bird societies of Japan, a park for cranes had been created. The 1960 meeting in Tokyo of the International Council for Bird Preservation, the leading international bird protection organization, had highlighted Japanese conservation efforts, and its resolutions, published and circulated in the nations of the world, had had great effect, including the initiation of a migratory bird treaty between Japan and the United States, and the focusing of attention on the danger that uncontrolled development represented for the great Japanese Crane. The U.S.A. had been making its own desperate efforts to save its Whooping Crane, and the U.S.S.R. and other Asian nations would soon follow suit with related species.

The cranes of the world are few in number of species, and all are now threatened by interference with their marshland breeding habitats as well as their long migratory flights, often over nations of hungry peasants now armed with rifles left over from wars both past and recent. Cranes are difficult to breed in captivity, and only a very few zoos or government laboratories and, preeminently, the International Crane Foundation in Baraboo, Wisconsin, have managed to unlock the secrets of crane reproduction. But in the twenty-one years that have elapsed since we witnessed the miraculous escape of that one Japanese Crane, the population of the species has perhaps trebled, from under five hundred to nearly thirteen hundred including many now breeding in captivity and a sizable number in China where data is still uncertain.

This fascinating volume, then, has an important story to tell us. Not only is the crane a feature of Japanese cultural tradition, an immemorial figure in literature, in myth, and in art, but its very existence today affords an encouraging lesson in the raising of consciousness about conservation and perhaps the moral obligation we all have to observe the fowls of the air and the creatures of the earth in their manifold passage upon the planet before their story ends, bringing intimations of our own demise.

We should all admire the persistence of cranes, their long life, their historical progression through the continents, knowing that, like the great creatures of the deep or the terrestrial animals about us, their lives and the ways they have found to adapt to life around them abound with lessons for us all, lessons yet unlearned, the moral yet unclear. The close interrelationship between the noble birds of Japan and its people should be a special lesson in this hurrying, careless age, a lesson teaching prudence as well as compassion.

S. Dillon Ripley
The Smithsonian Institution, 1981

2. White wings against the sky.

BALLERINA

Of all the world's cranes, Japan's red-crested crane—symbol of eternal youth and happiness—is certainly the most beautiful. The only crane in the world that winters in the cold north, this tall, stately bird is a dancer, a snow ballerina dressed in pure white with a black bustle and a cap of bright vermilion on a sleek head regally held high.

Most of the world's fourteen species of crane are gray. Only three are predominantly white, and they are the rarest; indeed, their conspicuousness against the summer greens may well have contributed to their depletion. And among these rare white birds—which include the Siberian White Crane (*Grus leucogeranus*), with its curious red face and whistling cry, and the Whooping Crane (*Grus americana*), only just recently saved from the brink of extinction—the Japanese Crane (*Grus japonensis*) is conspicuous for the perfection of its lines and the artistry of its plumage. For centuries an inspiration to local poets and artists, it has so captured the imagination of the Japanese people as a whole that, with the sun and the chrysanthemum, it has become a national emblem.

My admiration for this bird dates from my childhood, when I first learned to fold a paper crane. But my acquaintance with it was confined to its depiction in art and song and story until the photographer and naturalist Tsuneo Hayashida introduced me to living specimens in the wild. The first I ever saw were standing motionless in the crisp cold March air of a snow-covered field in the northern island of Hokkaido—a pair, secure in their disdain of a red fox running about in a stand of dark spruce not far away, on the other side of a stream. The fox, or perhaps a stag, had just sent the rest of the flock winging its way downstream, just before we arrived, with a piercing "*crew-whip, crew-whip, crew-whip, whip!*" that echoed across the snowy hills and could be heard over a mile away.

Graceful in flight, with the swift upbeat of their wings followed by a slow feathering of the air as they bring them down again, the grace of these birds on the ground, too, is astonishing. After all, swans are only beautiful

3. Fox and cranes (February).

◁ 1. Sunlight gilding a flight of cranes.

in flight or waterborne. Without exaggeration, the Japanese Crane seems incapable of any ungainly movement, whether in the air or merely pecking in a frozen cornfield.

The crane owes its princely presence partly to its height. Adult Japanese Cranes stand a meter and a half—nearly five feet—tall, as tall as some human beings. To primitive man they must have seemed creatures from another world, emerging mysteriously from treacherous peat bogs and swamps where people dared not go. At times uncannily human, yet seeming to know the secret of almost boundless life, it is no wonder these birds were thought to be divine. Japan's aboriginal Ainu called them "the marsh gods."

LONGEVITY AND HAPPINESS

The crane is a long-lived bird. Records exist of a crane living eighty years or more in a zoo—this in addition to whatever its age was when captured (a statistic impossible to determine accurately in adult birds). The estimated life of a crane in the wild, with all its hazards, is from thirty to fifty years, though its full potential is unknown.

In their ignorance of the bird's true lifespan, the Japanese imagined that cranes lived a thousand years, and together with the tortoise, which was said to live ten thousand years, the crane became a symbol of longevity.

Chinese mythology also celebrates the bird's endurance, for references in the ancient classics describe it as the bird-chariot of the immortal sages, who were transported on its wings. Even Japanese place-names sometimes commemorate the crane's longevity. In olden times, flocks of cranes used to congregate in the shallows of a river near Sapporo, Hokkaido's capital; instead of the predictable "Crane River," it was called Chitosegawa—the "River of a Thousand Years." (Sapporo's airport is at Chitose now, harboring winged creatures of a different kind.)

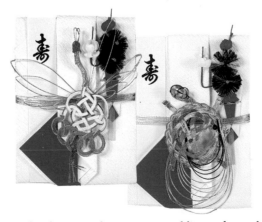

4. Stylized crane and tortoise on wedding cash envelopes.

Cranes are monogamous, pairing for life, and they are devoted mates in all seasons; as a result, not surprisingly,

11

they have also come to symbolize marital fidelity and love. They share their domestic tasks equally. They pamper their young and rear them with vigilant concern; and the degree of their parental devotion is reflected even in an old Japanese saying: "Like a crane at night and a pheasant on a burning moor."

For these reasons, the Japanese Crane is considered a bird of happiness and good omen, used frequently as a good luck symbol. Wedding kimonos usually have cranes embroidered on them, as do quilts and square wrapping cloths (*furoshiki*) given as wedding presents to wish the recipients a long life and a happy marriage. At New Year and on other felicitous occasions, a traditional ballad called *Tsurukame*, "The Crane and the Tortoise," used often to be sung and danced to samisen accompaniment; and though it is performed less frequently now, several popular folksongs sung at parties contain verses on the crane and tortoise theme.

5. Wedding kimonos.

WHAT IS A CRANE?

Few citizens of Japan today have actually seen living specimens of their crane, but illustrations of the bird are so common and its place in everyday life is so assured that there must be scarcely a soul not intimately familiar with its appearance.

Alas, this is not so in the English-speaking world. A middle-aged American couple I know, having a drink one day in a Tokyo hotel, were intrigued by the ornate plastic cranes decorating the end of the sticks holding the olives in their martinis. They lost no time in finding out where they were made, and, come Christmas, they sent their friends half a dozen each of these novelties.

To their dismay, no one recognized the species. "Thank you for the cute little seagulls," wrote one. "What darling little birds," wrote another, playing safe. And to their embarrassment, many of their friends sent congratulations, adding: "What an original way of announcing the happy event"!

Many Westerners confuse cranes with storks. Admittedly, storks are also fairly large and, like the Japanese Crane, predominantly white. But storks and cranes are not really similar at all: their habits readily distinguish them. True cranes (those of the genus *Grus*) are wading birds that build their nests on the ground, while storks build theirs high up, on treetops, electricity poles and, in Europe, chimney pots. Storks are much stockier than cranes, with thicker necks and bigger and broader bills, which they use for their characteristic clattering and hissing—for they have no song, as cranes do. Herons and egrets somewhat resemble cranes, but most are far smaller—only about half their size—and fly with necks bent, not stretched out in the manner of cranes.

Cranes are large, long-legged, long-necked, long-billed birds, and among the oldest on this planet. Crane bones nine thousand years old have been found in Japan in shell mounds (prehistoric refuse heaps) in Chiba, across the bay from Tokyo, and bones three to four thousand years old are fairly common throughout central and northeastern Japan. On the North American continent their presence is longer established: nine-million-year-old fossils of the Sandhill Crane in its present form have been found in Wyoming, and those of an extinct genus dating back five or six times that—to the Eocene Age—were discovered in Nebraska. Tomb drawings also reveal that the ancient Egyptians reared cranes in captivity.

There are fourteen kinds of crane (some ornithologists identify fifteen, dividing the colorfully bizarre African Crowned Cranes into two separate species), and with the exception of South America and Antarctica, cranes are found in all the continents of the world. Australia, India, North America, Europe, and Asia all have varieties of crane, and three island countries are also so endowed: Papua New Guinea, Cuba, and Japan.

But, sadly, with the steady encroachment of human activity upon their habitats, cranes have been driven into the few remaining wildernesses left. And few of us can ever see them now. . . .

6. Detail on a 1st-century Japanese bronze bell.
7. Taking off on a winter morning.

THE HABITAT

The Japanese Crane breeds in the marshlands of Tokachi, Kushiro, Nemuro, and Abashiri in the eastern region of Hokkaido. Originally nearly 30,000 hectares (about 75,000 acres) in size, Kushiro Marsh—its chief habitat—was free from human interference until recently. Now only about two-thirds its former area, it is still Japan's largest peat marsh and from December to April is almost completely frozen over.

Marshes are ideal nesting places for cranes, as the reedy vegetation grows tall and thick, hiding nests from view, and the soft, wet nature of the land makes it virtually inaccessible to man and beast alike.

When the marshes are frozen in winter and cushioned with snow, it is possible to penetrate them on skis and sleds, but once the thaw has begun, man sets foot there at his peril. In marshlands of the extreme north such as these, the ground consists of spongy masses of water plants piled layer upon layer over the centuries. The cold prevents the vegetation from decomposing.

Various rivers and innumerable tributaries meander in and out among these spongy beds, creating a multitude of islands. And as summer approaches, duckweed covers much of the water like grass, making it look deceptively safe underfoot but waiting to give the unwary a chest-high dunking. Small boats called *choro* can only negotiate these waterways with difficulty.

Even in April the vegetation is still mostly a vast jungle of dead stalks of *kitayoshi*, "reeds of the north" (*Phragmites communis*). These form dense, tall stockades—some more than two meters high—and unless seen from a high hill or a helicopter, nests are effectively concealed to all but other birds' eyes.

A CRANE IS BORN

Snow is still about and streams are still partially frozen when spring comes to the marshes of Hokkaido with the yellow blossoms of the wild Amur Adonis, a kind of pheasant's-eye. This is when the cranes begin to return in pairs from the winter feeding grounds, about three weeks after copulation; and they remain in their marshland wilderness until September and October, well away from man's inquisitive eye.

A pair's first task is to make a clearing on one of the islands in their marsh. Together, they pull up the dead stalks of reed and sedge with their beaks, and trample down the ground to make a smooth base. On this they build a nest, about a meter in diameter, mainly of dry reeds, but also sometimes sedge and twigs from alder trees that grow on some of the low hills surrounding the

8. Kushiro Marsh. ▷

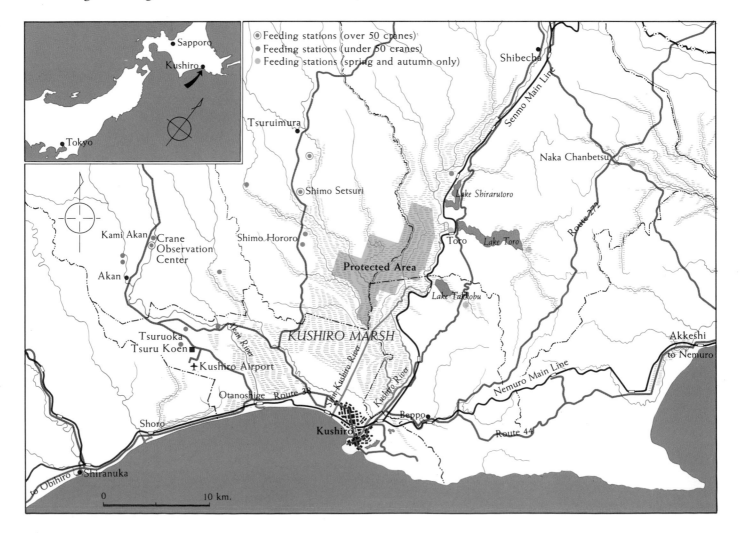

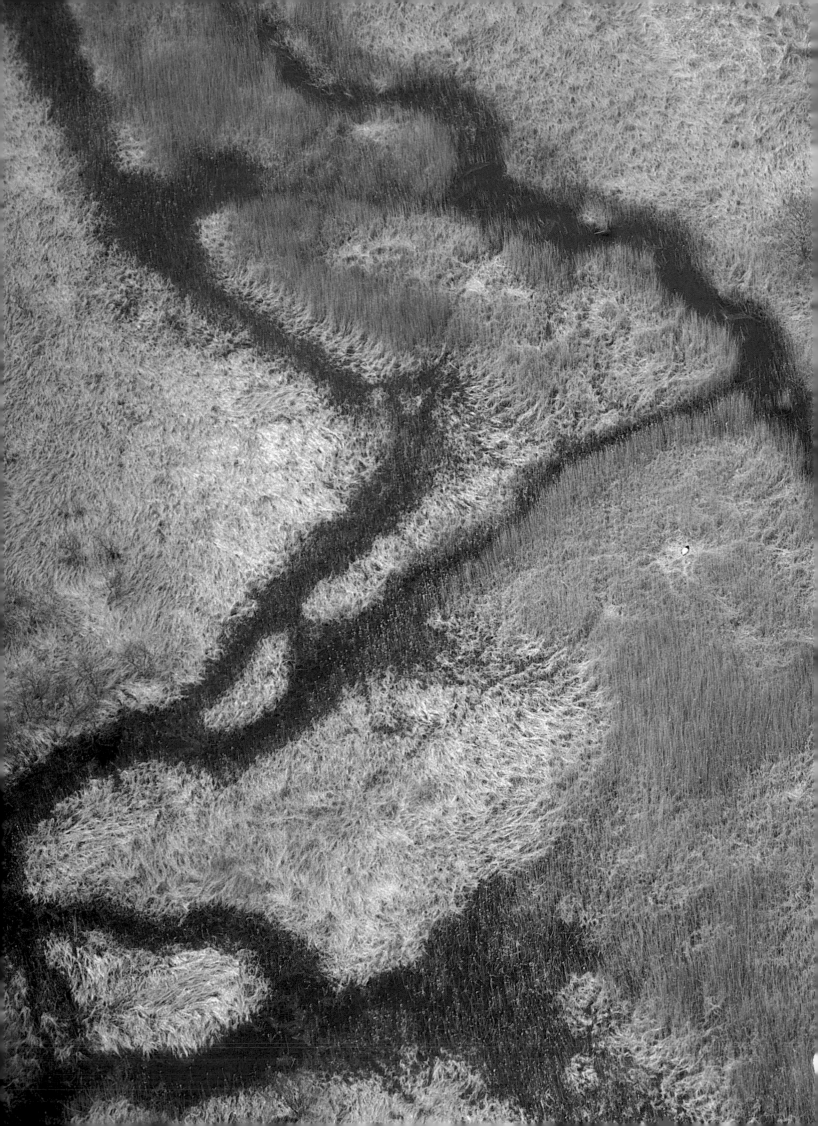

marshes. The nests often become entwined with growing reeds. One nest as large as two meters across was once found in a clearing twenty meters wide.

While they work on their nest together, sharing the labor equally between them, the cranes fly back each day to their feeding place to eat. Nest-building takes about a week. When the site is ready, the female lays its eggs—usually two. The eggs are twice as large as a hen's and four times heavier. Some are milk white, others a pale wine color, speckled in brown or gray. Most cranes' eggs are pitted and pimpled, but those of the Japanese Crane are smooth.

The female lays its eggs early in the morning, usually around six-thirty. And it will lay them sometime between the last week in March and the middle of May, depending on the lateness of the thaw. It lays its second egg usually two days after the first.

Just as they shared the work of making the nest, the pair share the duties of incubation too, one sitting on the eggs while the other flies off to feed. They change places at least twice a day and sometimes as often as four times. At night the female normally stays on the nest. The male sometimes moves back to their habitual winter roosting river, which may be as far as five kilometers away, but may spend the night at various locations in the marsh.

The incubating parent will stand up from time to time to roll the eggs over with its beak: it does this to keep the eggs evenly warm so the chicks inside will develop

◁ 9. Nest-building (April).

10. Meltwater threatens a hummock. Male on nest.

11. Male arriving to take its turn incubating.

12. *Adonis amurensis.*

13. Female rolling its eggs over with its beak.

properly. Incubation usually takes from thirty to thirty-five days.

Two or three days before hatching—generally sometime early in May—a chick begins to peck a hole in its eggshell. Once hatched, the chicks remain in the nest for several days, after which the parents lead them to drier areas near the edge of the marsh to feed. For about two months, the young birds sleep at night under the wings of the sitting female.

Parents do not have to worry about their offspring falling into the water: chicks are able to swim when only two or three days old; they are also capable of picking up their own food even on the day they are hatched, though their parents seem to prefer doing it for them, and one will guard the chick while the other forages in the near vicinity. By its third month, however, a young crane can fly, allowing the family to extend its range of feeding activity.

Seldom, alas, do both eggs hatch. In spite of the parents' vigilance, crows occasionally swoop down and carry one off, or the nest may become waterlogged after a downpour. When an egg does hatch it is an occasion for rejoicing, but watchfulness must continue, for chicks, too, are liable to be carried off by crows. Kites, buzzards, marsh harriers, and white-tailed sea eagles also pose a threat, as do brown bears, foxes, minks, raccoon dogs and snakes, although adult cranes can chase them all away. Cats and dogs turned wild can be more of a nuisance; but the crane's only serious enemy is man.

Appealing balls of tawny down at birth, crane chicks soon develop a plumage of light and dark browns and grays that afford them ample protection: their coloring blends in well with the background of last year's withered sedge and reeds. Only at the point where their wings join their bodies does a white spot presage the snowy brilliance to come. Traces of brown, beige, and gray remain among their plumage for two or three years, and black tips adorn the white primary feathers at the extremities of their adolescent wings. The beige head and neck of young cranes, and their lack of a red crest, easily distinguish them from adult birds.

For about ten months the chicks remain in the safekeeping of the parent birds. But as that first year draws to a close, the parents start pecking at their offspring and spurning their advances, then abruptly desert them altogether, to fly back to the marshlands to breed an entirely new generation.

Left behind on the winter feeding grounds, the yearlings congregate for company, and April finds them still there, gratefully accepting the farmers' corn as the snow gradually begins to melt. A few older cranes that have not yet found mates will be amongst them. In the following months, the birds move on to the marshes, and

14. Chick listening to peeps from a perforated second egg (May). ▷

often make a nuisance of themselves by trespassing on the territories of mated pairs.

By their second year, the birds undergo the annual summer molt of flight feathers which leaves all cranes unable to fly for about a month and, consequently, unduly nervous and wary.

Cranes mature at the age of four or five, then mate for life. They seem to breed year after year, but no one yet knows how long they can go on doing this.

WHAT DO CRANES EAT?
Cranes are omnivorous. The wild plant foods Japanese Cranes seem most to enjoy are the parsley-like dropwort (*seri*) and reed buds, but they will also eat cultivated vegetation such as cabbage, carrots, corn (maize), and buckwheat. However, their favorite treat in summer and spring is probably the small eel-like *dojo*, a kind of loach or mudfish. In Japan, where broiled eels are considered a delicacy, the plebeian equivalent is stewed loach, a sort of "poor man's eel," and both are rich in oils and nourishment. Cranes also like crucian carp and sticklebacks. Insects are high on their menu too, as are tadpoles, frogs, and an occasional salamander. It is possible that they also eat mud snails, dragonflies, and lampreys, as well as reed-warbler and mallard chicks, and small mammals such as moles and mice. Detailed analysis of what Japanese Cranes eat has not so far been possible, since live cranes feeding in the wild can only

15. Pair of cranes protecting their chick from a kite.

16. Pair foraging in Kushiro Marsh (July). ▷

be observed at a distance, and by the time scientists receive dead specimens through the complex government process now involved, the birds are too old for satisfactory inspection.

In early autumn the cranes return to the recently harvested fields and forage for grains of buckwheat and corn as well as insects and worms. And as winter wears on, they will willingly accept any corn put out for them by farmers and schoolchildren at designated feeding sites. Domestic corn is usually given to them on the cob, and when the cobs are empty, the birds like to kick the husks about and hoist them in the air. Most of the corn they get nowadays, however, is imported for feed and has already been scraped off the cob.

When feeding, cranes are obliged to first pick up a morsel of food with the tip of their bill and toss it slightly, catching it again further down the bill, nearer the gullet. Cranes need water, too, of course, and in autumn and winter, while feeding, they frequently fly back to their roosting river for a drink, though sometimes they will make do with snow.

FEEDING THE CRANES

Feeding the cranes was begun in 1952. That year Hokkaido was hit by an unusually harsh winter, with centigrade temperatures plummeting to thirty below zero. Desperate for food, cranes appeared for the first time this century in cultivated fields near human habitations, pecking at corn stacks and foraging for

18. Twenty-two-day chick with a minnow.

◁ 17. Parent feeding a five-day-old chick.

19. Trying to fly at two and a half months.

20. Returning to a farm in October. Mt. Me-Akan is behind.

21. Parents and two offspring on pasture near Tsuruimura.

grains left behind at harvest time. Their unprecedented appearance made the headlines and aroused great interest. As a result, the children of Naka-Hororo Primary School near Tsuruimura and Akan Middle School bought corn and buckwheat for the hungry cranes, and though initially unapproachable, the birds gradually became tame enough to accept this "charity." Money was donated for the project from all over the nation.

The following winter, the cranes returned, although temperatures were back to normal. Observers noted with surprise and delight that there were nine more birds than the thirty-three counted the year before.

Feeding continues now each winter, and the number of cranes has gradually increased to 272 (counted in December 1980). The primary school had to close down for lack of pupils, but a number of other places, mostly farms, were designated as winter feeding stations. The school-children's participation now mainly takes the form of bird-counting, and every year coordinated groups of students make valuable systematic records.

At Akan, a hundred kilometers northwest of Kushiro, a vegetable farmer who had put out corn for the cranes for many years sold a large tract of his land in 1977 to the municipal authorities, who built a fine observation

center there. The cranes are still fed at this site, oblivious to the serried ranks of cameras set up behind the boundary fence by both shutterbugs and bird watchers. They are intelligent birds, and know that the strangers are rigorously kept to their own side of the fence. But the farmer, who also manages the center, wryly observed that it was the visitors from down south who gave him the most trouble; Hokkaido people, he said, were generally interested in preserving their natural heritage.

At Tsuruimura (literally, "The Village Where Cranes Are"), fifty kilometers east of Akan, Tsuneo Hayashida and I watched about forty birds pecking in the snow for grains of corn that had been scattered there earlier by Mrs. Watanabe. There was a small tin-roofed hut with windows from which we gazed out at the cranes in relative comfort as they foraged, no more than a dozen or so meters away.

The snow was beginning to fall quite hard as daylight waned. Cheery, bright-faced Watanabe-san came out of her farmhouse as we watched, to scatter more feed. Some leaping high in the air, the adult cranes greeted her approach with high-pitched, unrestrained delight. "Cur-

22. Young crane tossing a corn husk.

24

LEW, *cur-LEW, cur-LEW!*" they cried. And the yearlings, almost as large as their elders but still waiting for their voices to break, peeped their pleasure as the countrywoman tossed handfuls of imported corn onto the snow. "Here you are! Come on now," she encouraged. "Eat it all up!" They allowed her right in amongst them.

"They're just like children to me, you know," she told us.

Mrs. Watanabe's husband is a member of a patrol that keeps Hokkaido's roads in good repair. It is she who is the farmer. In the typical barn, with its mansard roof—the sort one sees all over Japan's northern island—she rears, in summer, about ten head of cattle for the winter market. But with time on her hands during the snowbound months, she concerns herself with the cranes that flock to her paddock for food each day.

There are about thirty feeding stations like Mrs. Watanabe's. Cranes "patronize" them in numbers varying from pairs to flocks of between forty and eighty birds. Most of these sites—snow-covered all winter—are vegetable farms, cornfields, or grazing meadows from May to October. Some are partly used in winter, too, as exercise areas for cows and horses, but the cranes seem not to be disturbed by the presence of the animals or of nearby farmhouses. Pastures, though, have begun to encroach on some of their summer breeding grounds as well—something they are less likely to tolerate.

Crane families (or childless pairs) leave the marshes

23. Schoolchildren scattering corn (December).

24. Cranes foraging among stacked corn not far from Mt. O-Akan.

25. Flock descending on a feeding station at Akan. ▷

sometime between September and November. But before flying to the artificial feeding stations, they usually spend a period at some halfway river or pond to feed on its denizens, then move on to cornfields to glean the harvest leftovers. And when the ground begins to freeze, making most of their natural food unobtainable, pairs and families and single cranes form into two or three large assemblies and several smaller flocks and foregather at the usual farms.

TO SLEEP

The word "roost" usually suggests a perch of some sort. Indeed, the original Middle English word did mean a perch for fowls—specifically the rafters inside a roof—and comes from the Gothic *hrot*, a roof.

Most wild birds sleep perched in trees offering protection from predators on the ground and in the skies, but with the exception of females incubating eggs and sheltering chicks, cranes sleep standing up, usually in or near running water, with their bills tucked into their feathers. Not much is known about where cranes roost in summer as they do not seem to keep to specific places, but it is thought they sleep near water and among clumps of shrubs.

In winter they sleep on sandbars or in river shallows in the lee of a hill or high riverbank for shelter from the wind. Surrounded by water, they are safe from most four-footed beasts of prey, and in freezing weather the rivers offer relative warmth, for even in very cold climates some channels never freeze, and the water is several degrees warmer than the sub-zero night air. In winter, cranes usually gather in flocks to roost, although some families remain aloof for some reason and have their own spots. Roosts lie generally about two kilometers away from the feeding stations.

At daybreak the cranes begin to stir, and move their wings. Some will fly up onto level ground nearby and preen there for several hours before moving on, while some fly directly to a feeding ground. Daytime flights to and from the river tend to be in pairs and families, but they may leave initially and also return in fairly large flocks, flying in typical "V" or line formation.

Cranes roost standing on one leg, presumably to keep the other warm. They sometimes do this on snow-covered feeding and preening grounds as well. From time to time they alternate the leg, always giving the one they are raising a little shake before tucking it under their breasts.

During the night, they stir and look around from time to time, keeping a wary eye out for intruders. Once aware of any threat to a roost, moreover, the flock will abandon it for many months. Crane wardens are especially vigilant in trying to prevent overenthusiastic photographers from disturbing cranes in the winter rivers where they spend the night.

27. Sunrise: vapor rising from the river.

28. Cranes resting on a snowfield.

◁ 26. Akan River roost at dawn.

29. Settling down for the night under a full moon. ▷

30

THE VOICE OF THE CRANE

With the exception of the Crowned Cranes of Africa, cranes have resounding voices that carry for miles. One theory is that the greater the territorial needs, which are governed by the availability of food, the louder the vocal power.

Most cranes are provided with an extraordinary trachea, or windpipe, which is over a meter long; two-thirds of it is contained inside the breastbone in bends and coils rather like a trumpet or a horn. The crane's notes are musical, and mostly in the treble register. A multitude of cranes of various species landing or taking off in migration sounds like the wind section of an immense orchestra tuning up.

One of the most common calls of the Japanese Crane sounds to my ears like the name of another wading bird: "*Cur-LEW, cur-LEW, cur-LEW,*" or, more accurately, like the name of that bird in French, again heavily accenting the second syllable: "*Cour-LIEU, cour-LIEU, cour-LIEU.*" As the sun climbs over the hilltops, lighting the snowy crest of distant Mt. Me-Akan, cranes "halloo [this] name to the reverberate hills." It is a slow, leisurely call, sounded at various times during the day, sometimes exultant, sometimes merely announcing their arrival at the feeding ground. At times it sounds like: "Crew, will you?"

There is another, more urgent call: "*Crew-whip, crew-whip, crew-whip, whip!*"—rapid and lively, a variation of one or more of the following stanzas:

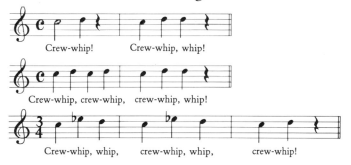

Crew-whip!   Crew-whip, whip!

Crew-whip, crew-whip,   crew-whip, whip!

Crew-whip, whip,   crew-whip, whip,   crew-whip!

But the crane's most fascinating call of all is the duet sung from time to time by husband and wife. Both birds gracefully arch their necks and point their bills skyward. And except when duetting at the nest, they raise their folded wings above their backs, the extent varying and sometimes barely perceptible, though the male almost always holds its feathers higher than its mate's and tosses them lightly in time to its song. They will sometimes face each other, or stand back to back, their pose a *pas de deux* of striking beauty as they sing this short antiphonal duet over and over again:

Male: "*Whee!*"
Female: "*Cock-cock.*"
Male: "*Whee!*"
Female: "*Cock-cock.*"

30. Resting, with neck bent.

31. Duetting.

32. Posing tensely, bills in air.

33. Mating: the female turns its back and spreads its wings.

34. Male jumps on its mate with a loud cry.

35. Copulation takes from four to eight seconds.

36. Male slides down over the female's head.

37. Arching exuberantly.

38. Cranes arch to impress both mate and trespasser.

39. Opening wings in a menacing gesture.

In the cold winter air the visible condensation of their breath makes it quite clear which bird is uttering which part of the call. One strong white puff from the beak of the male is followed immediately by two (sometimes three) short puffs from the female's bill.

In autumn, winter, and spring, the duets are performed a great many times and for many reasons. The pair may perform them to intimidate intruders, to advertise their territory, or immediately after copulation. Above all, they serve to strengthen the bond between two birds or to stimulate and synchronize the reproductive urge. And when one pair start, other pairs will often begin duetting too—a pretty thing to both see and hear.

These duets (or "unison calls" as some ornithologists dub them) are often sung during incubation, too, when one parent takes over the sitting duty from the other. And when another pair, several kilometers away, hear them, they will often answer, and the call will be taken up here and there by nesting pairs all over the marsh. A full-throated duet is also sung to announce the successful hatching of an egg.

Another call is the low "*crook, crook, crook*" with which parents encourage their chicks. Sometimes it is only a gentle "*purr.*" A single short quick "*crook*" is also often uttered by the leader of a group of cranes before taking flight.

A male will make a romantic suggestion to its mate with an almost inaudible "*crook, crook*," posing tensely, bill in air, before walking slowly away. The female follows, then turns its back on the other and spreads its wings. Just before the male mounts its mate it utters a sharp, persistent "*crook, crook!*" and its cries continue during copulation, rising in pitch and volume, then ceasing abruptly when it is over.

Chicks start to make themselves heard three days before hatching. Their tiny peeps develop a sort of miniature trill and become more of a "*peerr.*" Young cranes keep this voice until they are almost yearlings, even though in size they are scarcely distinguishable from their parents. Their trachea apparently takes a whole year to develop its resonance.

The voice of the adult crane is stridently authoritative and can be heard over almost any kind of din. Sitting in the coffee shop of the Crane Observation Center at Akan, I could hear it clearly at intervals over the hubbub, and thought of the Japanese expression *tsuru no hitokoe*—literally, "the single cry of the crane"—the voice of authority that silences a dispute.

When, in 1945, the Emperor informed his undecided cabinet that it was his wish that Japan should surrender, his pronouncement was referred to as "The Voice of the Crane."

PROUD, TERRITORIAL

The Japanese Crane is acquisitive, with a high degree of proprietary pride, and seems at pains to preserve a sense of authority in its bearing. In order to provide adequate food for its family it will seek to establish as broad a marsh territory as possible (which can be maintained with ease for years); and at feeding sites, which it is obliged to share with numerous competitors, it will try to monopolize all the corn it can by threat and intimidation. Both circumstances result in contention. Churchill once said that "you cannot add to your dignity by standing on it," but Japanese Cranes, when they puff out their feathers and swell their bright red crests, truly appear to add to their stature. Close contact is resented—sometimes even from a mate—and even very young birds object to being jostled and crowded. Family groups are expected to keep a distance of at least two meters and preferably three when feeding and roosting. Menacing gestures are made at individuals that fail to observe this etiquette. And while a male may even peck at its mate should the latter accidentally jostle it, if another crane comes too close the male will react with aggressive jealousy.

In asserting and defending its claims, *Grus japonensis* is prepared if necessary for violent conflict. Its sharp toes are deadly weapons, and bill and wings can be used as well. When attacking, the crane arches its neck and points its bill downward—displaying its red crest like a war emblem—before rushing its opponent. Cranes can easily throw an enemy off balance simply by flapping their wings, and they have been known to kill by piercing the other's skull with their bill. But extreme measures are seldom necessary: a threatening gesture is usually all that is required to send an intruder on its way, be it bird or beast. (It is worth noting that most of this defensive behavior is undertaken by the male.)

40. Cranes in combat.

41. Arching. ▷

42. The dance: bowing.

THE DANCE

The dance of the crane is one of the most wonderful sights in the bird world. Few people today have had the privilege of seeing it, and yet it must once have been a commonplace event the world over in the far-off days when nature was still largely untrammeled. The ancient Greeks are known to have had a crane dance imitating the bird's amazing leaps and pirouettes. In fact, Plutarch, writing in the second century, tells of how Theseus and his men performed it on the island of Naxos to describe the intricate twists and turns of the Minoan labyrinth from which they had just returned triumphant.

There is a crane dance in an old Noh drama, *Gekkyuden* (The Moon Palace), from which the congratulatory ballad "The Crane and the Tortoise" was adapted over a century ago. The play opens with a court banquet celebrating spring. The chorus describes the beauty of the imperial garden, and a courtier then informs the emperor that it is time for the annual crane dance, after which the court dancers will perform. Young boys always dance the roles of the crane and the tortoise—"old as the pines and the bamboo grove"—to the sound of flute and drum. The emperor himself then dances "to bring prosperity to all the land forever."

Japan has a city called Dancing Crane. In fact, Maizuru is named after the castle that once stood in its midst; the Japanese were presumably so familiar with the crane's exuberant dance that their feudal castles with gleaming white walls surmounted by tier upon tier of upswept dark-tiled roofs reminded them of the dancing bird.

The aboriginal Ainu of Hokkaido still live in crane country, and their own traditional crane dance is still

43. Leaping.

38

performed. Since this marvelous bird was, to them, *sarorun kamui*, "the marsh god," the Ainu's slow pavane is a kind of sacred rite—a charm against evil.

In the version danced today in Tokachi and along the Ishikari River near Sapporo, two young girls miming a pair of cranes posture around a child seated on the ground, who represents their chick and eventually spreads its "wings" and flies away. In the Kushiro version, the dancers raise the hems of their rough cotton kimonos high above their heads like wings, shaking and rustling the dark blue, geometrically patterned cloth to ward off bad spirits. Originally, it is said, they used this technique to scare bears away, in deference to the crane's own effective tactics, which earned it a reputation among the Ainu as a "bearbaiting bird."

Only women, incidentally, perform the Ainu crane dance; the men are traditionally supposed to remain in-

44. "Treading air."

45. Whirling.

46. Friendly chasing.

doors. And a chorus of women surrounds the dancers, clapping rhythmically and imitating the bird's cries in their refrain: "*Ah-HAW, ah-HAW, HAW.*"

In Australia, too, the aborigines—their naked bodies whitened with clay—dance in a ring imitating the movements of their Brolga, or Australian Crane (*Grus rubicunda*). Indeed, the crane's extraordinary terpsichorean display seems to enthrall all who are fortunate enough to be familiar with it.

All cranes seem to love dancing. They bounce and leap and whirl about, first bobbing, then with heads held high, wings gracefully spread. They sometimes begin by picking up objects with their bill and throwing them in the air several times, following this with bounces. Their leaps can be two or three meters high, and they can remain airborne for moments by spreading their wings and "treading air" with their legs. The effect is comic at times, but still graceful. These bounces and leaps are the basis of their dance.

Cranes dance at any time of day, in any season, and at any age. A Sandhill Crane hand-reared in Michigan is reported to have danced all over the garden—bobbing its head, leaping, and tossing objects in the air—when barely six days old! Cranes dance in pairs and singly. They seem to dance as much from pure *joie de vivre* as for more cogent reasons such as courtship. A pair often dance after copulation. Both may dance opposite one another, or one alone around the other: just before singing their duets, one crane often does a sort of flamenco move-

ment around the other, walking stiffly, neck straight and taut, with head down to show the red crest, and wings raised a little.

Japanese Cranes dance most in late winter and early spring—that is, from about January until the end of March. Apparently on impulse and usually while feeding, one of a pair of birds will suddenly look at the other and start bowing, bobbing its head. Its partner stops eating, turns to face it, and after a while begins bowing back. Presently, the first bird adds a few wing flaps to its head-bobbing, turning around the while with little dancing steps. The turns become faster, until the other bird joins its partner face to face and they begin leaping high in the air, flapping their wings, and floating down gently together after particularly high jumps. Sometimes in the course of the dance one may whirl around, turning its back on its partner and spreading wide its wings to display to the other the full panoply of its striking black and white markings.

When one pair of cranes start dancing together, other pairs frequently follow suit, and soon the field resembles a festival of folk dancers. Unmated cranes and yearlings often join in the fun, and those wanting a partner have even been known to "ask" a crow to dance! (Indeed, once in a while Japanese Cranes will even mate with cranes of other species—generally migrating stragglers that have landed in Japan on their own.)

47. Leaping up into wind-driven snow (February). ▷

AT CLOSE QUARTERS

The adult Japanese Crane is almost entirely snow-white, except for its black throat, lore (a strip between eye and bill), and neck; it also sports a handsome row of black feathers along the lower edge of its wings. The first sixteen of these are called secondaries and those next to the crane's body tertials. The tertials are pointed, hang rather loosely, and are capable of erection. When the crane folds its wings, the black feathers droop over the bird's short white tail, giving the impression that the crane's tail is black. Many of Japan's old prints and paintings give the crane a black tail in flight and a completely white wing, although as early as the seventeenth century an observer in Matsumae—Hokkaido's single feudal fief at the time—recorded the fact that the black feathers were not the tail. Artists and designers still make this mistake today!

It is the bare red patch on the crown of its head that gives the Japanese Crane its vernacular name, *tancho*, "red crest." This patch turns a brighter vermilion and swells in size at certain times, as when the bird is intimidating an opponent or intruder, or arousing a mate. On these occasions, the bird lowers its head to show off its bright emblem—so strangely reminiscent of the national flag—to best advantage.

The Japanese Crane has dark brown eyes, an olive-green bill, and grayish-black legs with scales resembling snakeskin—a relic, they say, of its reptilian origin aeons ago.

The sexes are similar, although the female is usually a little smaller than the male, weighing three to four kilograms less. *Grus japonensis* is among the largest members of the crane family, and males have been known to weigh as much as fifteen kilograms. Their length is, on average, 135 centimeters from the tip of the bill to the end of their short tail.

48–49. The red crest, which consists of bare, warty skin, grows larger and brighter when cranes are excited.

Cranes usually fly with their legs and necks stretched out, giving them a graceful symmetry in the air. But in very cold weather they are apt to tuck their legs in close to the body for warmth. And being large, heavy birds, they need to run for several paces into the wind in order to become airborne, flying with a characteristic uneven rhythm—a short, quick upstroke followed by a much slower downstroke.

Since Hokkaido's resident population of *Grus japonensis* moves only a few kilometers between winter feeding grounds and summer breeding marshes, they need not fly high or all together. Migrating flocks on the continent of Asia, however, would spiral up to heights of a mile or more and fly in large "V" formations.

50. Reptilian scales on gray-black legs.

WHAT'S IN A NAME?

To the Japanese people, the single word *tsuru*, "crane," invariably means the Japanese Crane, though its real name is *tancho*. When the word *tsuru* becomes a suffix, as in the Japanese names for the other species, the *ts* sound is softened to a *z*: the Hooded Crane (*Grus monacha*) and the White-naped Crane (*Grus vipio*)—still regular winter visitors in one or two spots in southern Japan—are called *nabezuru* and *manazuru* respectively.

Likewise, the Japanese themselves tend to call the Japanese Crane *tanchozuru*. But this is incorrect: the true vernacular designation is simply *tancho*, a name derived from the Chinese.

Confusion surrounds the name of this bird. Known as both the Japanese Crane and the Manchurian Crane in English, the Dutch call it a Chinese Crane, the Russians an Ussuriland Crane, the French a Montigny Crane, and the Germans a Manchurian Crane. This is hardly surprising, since there are two distinct populations of *Grus japonensis*.

One is the unique cold-weather resident population in Japan's northern island, and the other is a continental Asian population. Most of the latter breed in northern Manchuria and southeastern Siberia in the Sungari River and Lake Khanka regions. They migrate in winter to the northern part of South Korea and to eastern China, with the occasional bird or two finding its way to Taiwan or Kyushu, Japan's main southern island.

Japanese Cranes in local zoos—with the exception of the crane park in Kushiro—are all birds captured in Korea or China.

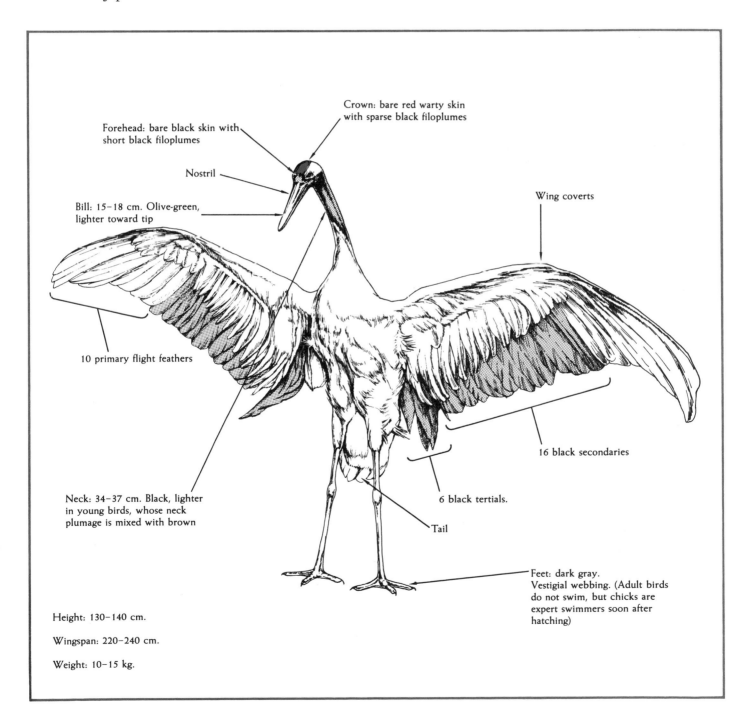

Crown: bare red warty skin with sparse black filoplumes

Forehead: bare black skin with short black filoplumes

Nostril

Bill: 15–18 cm. Olive-green, lighter toward tip

Wing coverts

10 primary flight feathers

16 black secondaries

6 black tertials.

Neck: 34–37 cm. Black, lighter in young birds, whose neck plumage is mixed with brown

Tail

Feet: dark gray. Vestigial webbing. (Adult birds do not swim, but chicks are expert swimmers soon after hatching)

Height: 130–140 cm.

Wingspan: 220–240 cm.

Weight: 10–15 kg.

51. Cranes usually fly with their neck and legs outstretched.

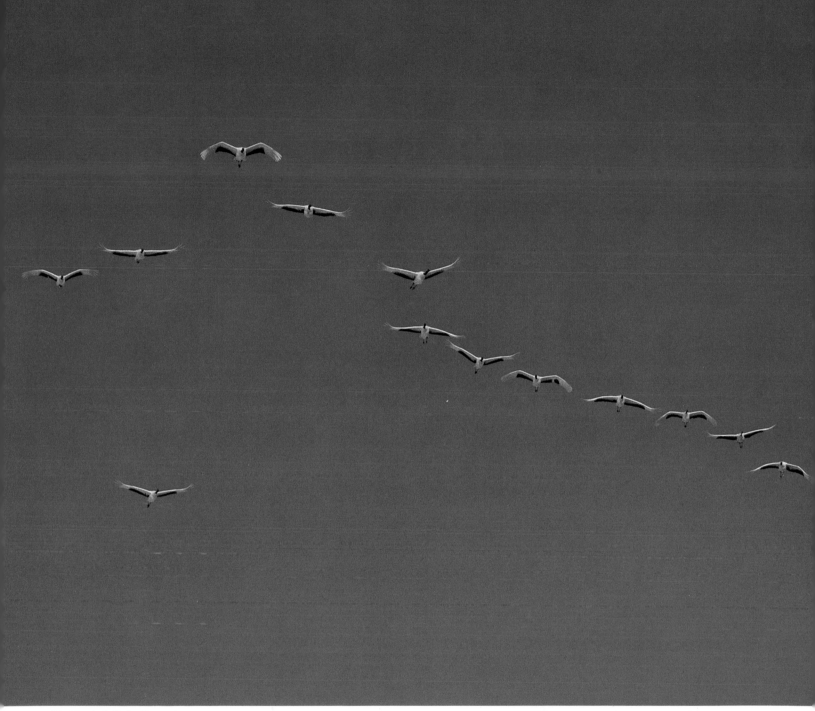

52. Typical flight formation.

53–57. Pair of cranes taking flight. Owing to their weight, cranes need to run at least ten meters into the wind with wings spread in order to become airborne.

47

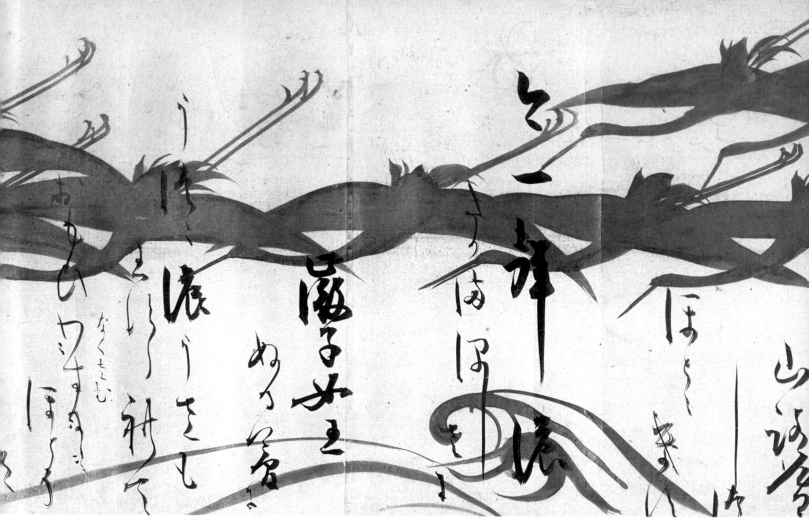

58. Detail of Sotatsu's myriad-crane masterpiece.

IN ART

The idea for the *senbazuru* or "thousand cranes" theme may have originated with the artist Sotatsu in 1611 in his famous fifteen-meter scroll of that title. On an animated background composition of a myriad cranes—some in flight and some at play on a seashore, some painted in silver leaf and some in gold—are poems by the thirty-six major classical poets of old Japan, inscribed in superb calligraphy.

Sotatsu's poetry scroll is considered to be his masterpiece; and the idea caught on. To Sotatsu's celebrated disciple Korin (1658–1716) is attributed a silk incense wrapper with the same thousand-crane motif, the cranes painted in Chinese white on a gold background—half of them overlaid in silver—with their tails, bills, and feet accented in black. Hiroshige, one of the nineteenth century's two most popular woodblock-print artists, also used this design on figured paper. And ever since, it has continued to be a popular motif in every conceivable medium.

Japanese art, especially from the fifteenth century onward, is filled with representations of the Japanese Crane, as well as the occasional migrant species of crane, although *Grus japonensis* is favored for its sentimental and auspicious associations. Cranes appear on hanging scrolls, door panels, screens, sword guards, ceramics, and prints, as well as textiles and lacquerware. Some were based on careful sketches of captive birds, and some, like Hokusai's

print of Umezawa in central Japan—part of a series executed between 1823 and 1830—were obviously inspired by scenes in the wild. The captive birds, however, would have been seen standing with folded wings, giving the impression that the black feathers were their tails,

59. Lacquer comb with a crane and young pines. Early 19th century.

and it is not surprising that most artists, despite painstaking attention to detail, got this part wrong. They include Harunobu (1725–70), a pioneer of the full-color print, whose charming *Courtesan on a Crane* reveals this error. (The print is part of a series in which beautiful women in contemporary dress were substituted for characters in Chinese mythology.)

Artistic interest in the crane theme shows no sign of flagging, and even Japan Air Lines contributes to its perpetuation in the stylized crane crest it uses as its emblem. Indeed, cranes have become legion as commercial trademarks, particularly for traditional products such as *sake*.

IN LITERATURE

Cranes appear frequently in ancient Japanese poetry. The *Manyoshu*, for example, an anthology compiled in the seventh and eighth centuries, contains many verses on the subject. In most of them, the crane's connubial cry is used to evoke in the poet a lonely nostalgia for a deceased lover or spouse.

One of the oldest poems in which the bird appears is a beautifully objective nature study of a scene that must have been common up and down Japan in those days. It is by Yamabe-no-Akahito, a courtier in the reign of Emperor Shomu (724–49) whose verses were so highly thought of that the emperor often commanded him to set down his impressions of well-known beauty spots.

Wakanoura, on the western shore of the Kii Peninsula, is a picturesque bay embracing a sandspit once luxuriant with pines. There were marshes near the shore in olden times, and the waters of the bay were so pristine that wading birds crowded the flats when the tide receded. Akahito's cranes were almost certainly *Grus japonensis*.

> When the tide comes in,
>   Flooding sandbars all along
>   Wakanoura's shore,
>   To the reedy marsh they fly—
>   Cranes, with their resounding cry.

The shorter form of Japanese verse—the haiku—owes much to the seventeenth-century wanderer-poet Basho.

In his *Narrow Road to a Far Province* he includes a verse about some cranes he saw standing in the lagoon shallows among the sand dunes at Shiogoshi, a spot meaning "tideway" on the Japan Sea coast.

> Cool seascape with cranes
>   Wading long-legged in the pools
>   Mid the Tideway dunes.

It is significant that Basho's haiku was written in summer, as it bolsters the theory that Japanese Cranes on the main island were then not just winter visitors from

60. Early 17th-century sword guard.

61. Crane in a resting pose by Motonobu (1476–1559) of the Kano school, painted on a door panel in the high priest's quarters, Reiun-in temple, Kyoto.

the Asian continent or Hokkaido, but resident birds, breeding over much of Japan.

There is a curious reference to cranes in the famous *Tosa Diary*, written in the year 936 by a former governor of Tosa Province on his way back to Kyoto, then Japan's capital. The work describes the journey by boat to Osaka from Kochi on the southern coast of the island of Shikoku.

The ex-governor's voyage in a sailing vessel equipped with oars took thirty-nine days. They were plagued with storms and often had to put in at various ports, waiting days for the weather to clear. The passengers passed the time writing verses describing the scenery and their thoughts en route.

After leaving a harbor called Ominato, they sailed past the pine-covered shores of Uta. The centuries-old trees stretched along the coast as far as the eye could see, and atop each one there perched a snow-white crane. Every time a large wave thundered against the beach, the birds took flight. The official and his companions watched in endless fascination, and someone wrote a charming verse imagining that each crane—a thousand years old—had accompanied its own pine tree for those lifelong years.

But the author's knowledge of natural history was somewhat inferior to his literary skill. From a distance, out at sea as they were, the large white birds may have looked like cranes, but they were obviously storks, for cranes never nest or even perch on top of trees. Storks (*konotori*) were once fairly common in Japan, but now are almost extinct.

In the same century, a noblewoman known only as Michitsuna's mother wrote a celebrated autobiographical work entitled the *Diary of a Mayfly*. One of the three outstanding beauties of her day, her marriage was nevertheless unhappy, and her loneliness is reflected poignantly in her writing, particularly her poems.

She writes of being asked to provide verses for a

63. Harunobu's *Courtesan on a Crane*.

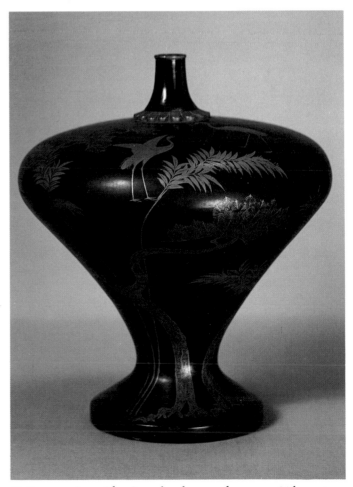

62. *Raku*-ware tea bowl. 18th century.

64. Lacquer jar with pines, bamboo, and cranes. 16th century.

65. Lid of lacquer box with lead and silver inlay. 18th century.

66. Kimono detail: cranes, pine, bamboo, and plum—symbols of good fortune. 19th century.

selection of pictures to be pasted on a screen for presentation to some important government minister on his fiftieth birthday. One of the paintings featured a popular congratulatory scene: a pine grove on a beach with cranes beneath the trees (in both literature and art, cranes as symbols of longevity are often paired with pines— hardy trees that live for hundreds of years). Two verses were required, the more to emphasize these two prime tokens of good fortune. She wrote:

> By the wild sea strand,
>   Where waves break upon the shore,
>   Young green pine trees stand.
> Each leans fondly toward the other—
> Loved and lover; child and mother.
>
> Neath each green pine tree,
>   Staring at the grains of sand
>   With such intensity,
> What can *you* so yearn to find?
> Cranes, you've soulmates of your kind!

Her lines about the cranes were apparently too wistful

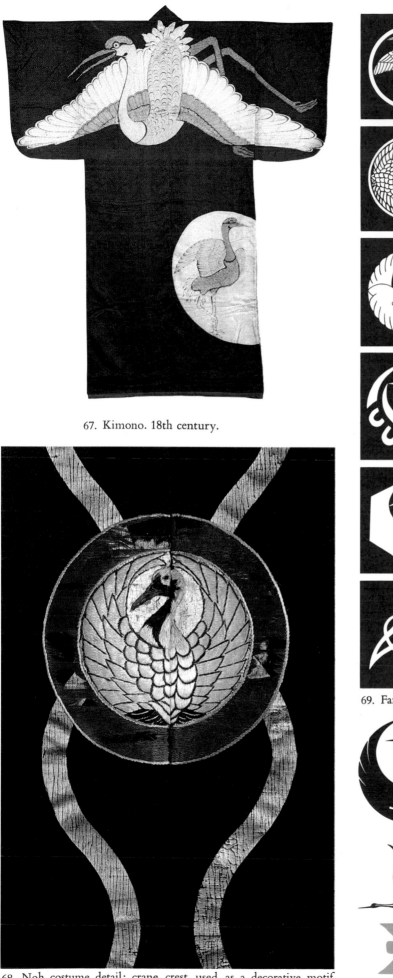

67. Kimono. 18th century.

68. Noh costume detail: crane crest used as a decorative motif. 19th century.

69. Family crests.

70. Commercial trademarks.

71. Kimono: embroidery and tie-dye. 19th century.

for the birthday occasion, for she records that they were not used.

Now, ten centuries later, cranes still feature prominently in Japanese literature. The novel *Thousand Cranes* by the late Nobel Prize-winning writer, Yasunari Kawabata, takes its title from the pattern on the square silk wrapper carried by a girl the hero meets at a tea ceremony. "One of the girls was beautiful. She carried a bundle wrapped in a kerchief, the thousand-crane pattern in white on a pink crape background." The hero thereafter associates the girl with cranes. As she performs the tea ceremony he sees "a thousand cranes, small and white, start up in flight around her."

FOLD ME A THOUSAND CRANES

Almost two hundred years ago, in 1798, a book was published in Kyoto called "How to Fold a Thousand Cranes." It shows in detail forty-nine ways of

72. *Origami* (folded paper) cranes.

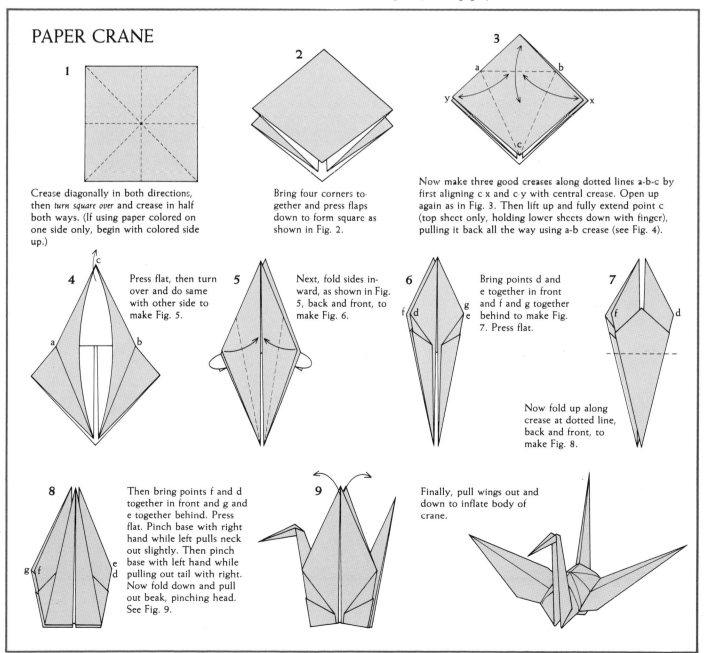

PAPER CRANE

1 Crease diagonally in both directions, then *turn square over* and crease in half both ways. (If using paper colored on one side only, begin with colored side up.)

2 Bring four corners together and press flaps down to form square as shown in Fig. 2.

3 Now make three good creases along dotted lines a-b-c by first aligning c x and c y with central crease. Open up again as in Fig. 3. Then lift up and fully extend point c (top sheet only, holding lower sheets down with finger), pulling it back all the way using a-b crease (see Fig. 4).

4 Press flat, then turn over and do same with other side to make Fig. 5.

5 Next, fold sides inward, as shown in Fig. 5, back and front, to make Fig. 6.

6 Bring points d and e together in front and f and g together behind to make Fig. 7. Press flat.

7 Now fold up along crease at dotted line, back and front, to make Fig. 8.

8 Then bring points f and d together in front and g and e together behind. Press flat. Pinch base with right hand while left pulls neck out slightly. Then pinch base with left hand while pulling out tail with right. Now fold down and pull out beak, pinching head. See Fig. 9.

9 Finally, pull wings out and down to inflate body of crane.

folding multiple birds from a single sheet of paper.

That is difficult enough, but to fold a thousand separate cranes and then thread them together in clusters, as is still popular with girls in Japan today, is no mean feat. The idea behind it is this: since cranes were thought to live a thousand years, the very act of folding a large number of paper ones was supposed not only to confer longevity on the folder, but to wish the recipient of his handiwork a long life and sustained good health.

In one prefecture in northern Japan, for example, the oldest member of the household is traditionally presented each year, in mid-summer, with a number of folded cranes equivalent to his or her age, on behalf of the rest of the family. But a more widespread custom is to make a garland of cranes from colored squares of paper for friends who are ill, to wish them a speedy recovery.

Strings of a thousand paper cranes are often hung from the rafters of temples and shrines, placed there as votive offerings to petition the deities not only for convalescence in illness, but for help in the attainment of feminine accomplishments and the fulfillment of various hopes and desires.

One of the most moving examples of the petitionary aspect of paper cranes can be seen at the Peace Park in Hiroshima. There stands a statue of a young girl holding in her hands, high in the air, a folded paper crane—a prayer, a yearning for peace. From the roof of the dome that shelters the monument hang hundreds of thousand-crane clusters made by visitors from all over the country.

The idea for the statue was conceived by the friends of a young victim of the atom bomb, struck down by radiation disease after the end of the war. While in hospital she began folding a thousand cranes in the hope of eventual recovery. Sadly, however, she died after finishing only five hundred and eight of her birds. Her school friends collected donations from the pupils of over three

THE CRANE-WIFE

LONG AGO, in the cold northeast of Japan, there lived a young man in a humble cottage at the edge of the woods, all alone. He had been orphaned at an early age, and he was very poor, scraping together a living gathering brushwood.

One day, as he was chopping branches up in the hills, a large white bird suddenly fell almost at his very feet. It flopped about, trying to raise itself, then lay quite still, exhausted.

"Well, upon my word, if it isn't a wounded crane!" he said to himself.

The poor helpless bird looked up at the young man with its soft brown eyes as he approached. He carefully lifted one wing, and found an arrow piercing its flesh. Gently drawing it out, he gathered up the great bird, which was almost as big as he. It tried to struggle a little, but then lay limply in his arms as he carried it to a stream not far away.

Laying the wounded bird on the bank, he cupped his hands and splashed cold, clear water on the wound, and bit by bit the congealed blood was washed away. After a while the crane appeared to rally a little, and made one or two feeble attempts to struggle to its feet. Finally it succeeded, and found to its joy that it could flap its wings. After standing still and resting for a while as the young man stood quietly watching, the crane ran a little way along the bank of the stream, facing into the breeze, and soon was in the air.

Circling several times above the young man's head, the crane gave a cry that sounded very much like, "*Thank-YOU, thank-YOU, thank-YOU!*" Higher and higher it circled before disappearing into the clouds.

The young man went back to his pile of brushwood and resumed cutting and chopping. But his axe now felt lighter than it ever had before.

"That was a good deed I did," he said to himself.

Not long afterward, he was working in the hills as usual, chopping brushwood, when a storm came on. Before long, he was drenched to the skin. Trudging home to his little cottage as darkness fell, he felt very lonely and forlorn. "How nice it would be," he thought, "if someone were waiting at home to welcome me."

It was almost dark as he turned the last corner of the winding path down the hill. He rubbed his eyes. Surely he must be dreaming. That couldn't be a light in his cottage. He wondered if he had taken a wrong turning. Could it be someone else's house?

As he hesitantly slid open the door, out from the kitchen came the most beautiful girl he had ever seen.

"How wet you are. You must be cold," she said.

He was sure now that he had come to the wrong house. It was dark outside and the lady must have mistaken him for her husband. But when he looked inside he knew it was his own house except that it was now spick and span, as neat as a pin. From the hearth came the appetizing smell of hot broth.

Smiling at his bewilderment the girl said shyly: "I hope you'll let me stay. I'd like to live with you and be your bride."

thousand primary and secondary schools throughout Japan to build the memorial.

IN LEGEND

Scholars of folklore have written a great deal about the myth of the swan-maiden. Sagas and fairy tales based on the theme of a bird turning into a lovely woman and becoming the wife of a mortal exist all over the world in one form or another. In fact, it is considered one of the most widely distributed and attractive stories ever invented by man.

In Europe, the bird is usually a swan—a creature whose grace aptly epitomizes the beauty and purity of the ideal woman. In Arabia, the bird is not specified, but in Finland it is a goose. In the Celebes and ancient Bohemia it is a dove, and in Guyana a king vulture.

One common variant of the tale involves, like Japan's *Hagoromo* story, not a bird but a supernatural maiden captured through retention of her feathered robe.

The tale very often includes a taboo of some sort, which, when broken, causes the divine creature to return to the heavens. Religious beliefs impose certain variations, too. Indian Buddhism is responsible for a variant concerning man's kindness to an animal and the animal's return of that kindness.

Both these elements are present in Japan's version of the swan-maiden theme. A poor but kind young woodcutter rescues a wounded crane, which repays his kindness by appearing as a beautiful girl who becomes his wife. Not only does she reward him with loving companionship and domestic help, but she aids him financially by sacrificing her own feathers and weaving of them a rare stuff, "cloth of crane feathers," for him to sell. But like all weak mortals, he breaks a taboo and loses her—by watching her at work and discovering her true identity.

Besides the crane-wife version, there is a crane-daughter

"But . . . but that's impossible! I can't afford a wife. I'm far too poor."

He blurted out the words, he couldn't help it. But she quickly reassured him.

"Money means nothing to me. Please let me stay."

The young man pinched himself to make sure he wasn't dreaming. She went on to tell him she was an orphan like himself, with nowhere to go. He was overjoyed to have her share his humble home, and they lived happily together for many, many moons.

One day she asked the young man to make her a loom so she could do some weaving. He chopped down a sturdy tree and made her a loom and a little hut to put it in. Delighted with his handiwork, she could hardly wait to begin. But first she made him promise not to look into the hut for seven days and seven nights until she had finished weaving.

For seven days and seven nights the valley and the hill echoed with the sound of her loom.

Crickety creak, thump.

Crickety creak, thump.

When the seven days and seven nights were over, the door of the hut opened and out came his bride holding in her arms a length of cloth so beautiful it took the young man's breath away. It was like nothing he had ever seen or even heard of in his life before. But he noticed with distress that she had become a great deal thinner, and he worried about it.

"Take this," she said, "and sell it in the town. But don't fix a price for it. The price should be decided by the buyer."

He nodded, while she went on: "While you're gone, I'll weave some more. If you return before I've finished, remember your promise not to look in."

The young man promised faithfully, and off he went with the bolt of cloth. Up seven hills and down seven dales he marched, till finally, at long last, he came to the castle town, and paused by the bridge that led over the moat to the great gate.

Many people stopped to look at the cloth and ask its price, but the young man remained silent.

"I'll give you five *ryo* for it," said one.

"Why, I'll pay twice that," said another.

"Nonsense," cried a third. "This cloth is worth at least thirty *ryo!*"

Just then, a samurai came out of the great gate and crossed the bridge to where the young man stood.

"This cloth isn't for common folk," he said. "Follow me." And he led the young man into the castle.

When the lord of the castle saw the material his eyes opened wide in amazement. Without a moment's hesitation he untied a silken purse and poured out a hundred shining pieces of gold.

variation, possibly tailored for children, avoiding the looseness of the marriage bond in the other tale. Coming from the island of Sado, it is called "The Gratitude of the Crane" and has a girl, who says she has lost her way, appearing out of the snow at the home of an elderly childless couple who are kind and good but very poor. The old man once freed a crane from a trap. The girl stays with the couple and is soon treated as a daughter by them. One day she asks them to buy her a skein of purple silk, which she weaves together with her feathers into "damask brocade." This takes her three days, as opposed to the other version's seven.

But again the good couple peer into the weaving chamber, not only out of curiosity but because they are worried: the weaving has taken so long and the girl become so thin. When discovered, the crane-daughter says she would have had to leave them eventually anyway, and the old couple adopt an orphan girl to take her place.

In his play *Yuzuru* (The Evening Crane), awarded the Mainichi Drama Prize in 1949, the contemporary playwright Junji Kinoshita develops the crane-wife story by introducing an element of human greed to illustrate a universal theme—the struggle between spiritual values and materialism. A pair of unscrupulous entrepreneurs manipulate a simple youth and persuade him to force his crane-wife to weave more and more "cloth of a thousand feathers" so they can sell it for enormous sums, of which the simpleton only gets a small portion.

Composer Ikuma Dan used Kinoshita's play as the libretto for Japan's most successful modern opera. *Yuzuru* is performed annually to enthusiastic audiences all over the country; indeed, it has become a regular event, and folk in remoter regions have even come to believe that the opera itself is as old as the fairy tale. Entitled *The Twilight Heron* in English, the opera has been performed in the United States as well as Europe.

"This, young man, is crane-feather cloth. Very rare indeed. I'll buy all you can bring me."

So overcome he could not reply, the young man merely bowed his head to the ground, and taking the hundred pieces of gold he returned home, walking on air. He could not remember crossing the first hill, or the second, or even the third. As for the fourth and fifth, he passed over them as if he were in a dream. When he finally reached the seventh dale he began to hear the sound of the loom:

Crickety creak, thump.

Crickety creak, thump.

It echoed across the valley from hill to hill.

"So my sweet wife is still busy a-weaving," he thought. And then he suddenly stopped. "That's strange. I'm certain she took no skeins of silk with her into the hut. How can she weave without any thread?"

The more he thought about it, the stranger it seemed to be.

When he reached his house he went in and sat down by the hearth. But he couldn't sit still. He opened his bag and counted the gold coins for the umpteenth time.

"When will she finish weaving," he wondered. He couldn't imagine how she could weave without any thread. And why did it make her so thin? Perhaps he ought to stop her from working so hard.

He got up and went toward the hut. Then he remembered his promise. Back at the hearth he sat down again. But it was no use. Finally his curiosity got the better of him.

He crept up to the hut and peered in through a crack in the door. What he saw almost made his heart stop beating. His bride was nowhere in sight. Seated before the loom was—a crane! With its long beak it was pulling out the last few feathers from its breast and placing them in the loom, all the while working the treadle with its feet.

Crickety creak, thump.

The young man staggered back to the house and broke out

in a cold sweat. Suddenly everything went dark. He lay on the floor for a long time.

By the time he came to, night had fallen, and his bride was bending over him, her face paler than before and her body pitifully thin. Beside her lay a bolt of crane-feather cloth, neatly folded.

"I am the crane you once rescued," she said. "But now that you know, I may no longer stay here with you. My only regret is that I couldn't stay long enough to weave you one more piece of cloth. Then you would never have wanted for money."

So saying, she gradually turned back into a bird—right there before his eyes—and, falteringly, ran out of the door on her slender little crane legs, gave a tiny jump, and flew off into the evening sky. As the crane circled higher and higher in the twilight glow, the young man thought he heard a sad, sad call: "*A-dieu! A-dieu! A-dieu!*"

NOW ONLY NAMES . . .
The familiar presence of cranes in many parts of Japan up to a century and a half ago is attested to by a number of widely scattered place-names. Besides Tsurumi (Crane View) and Tsurugamine (Crane Ridge) right outside Tokyo, there is Tsurugi (Cranes Come) in the hills behind Kanazawa on the Japan Sea coast. Kyushu, the chief southern island, has its Tsurusaki (Crane Cape) and Tsuruda (Crane Field), and throughout Japan one finds many a Tsuruoka (Crane Hill)—often spelled Tsurugaoka—although these sometimes take their name from the hilltop castle whose crane-wing roofs once dominated the town.

Not only did *Grus japonensis* probably breed throughout the land in marshes such as Oze in the central highlands of Nikko, but migrant Japanese Cranes from Asia as well as other continental cranes—mainly the dark gray *nabezuru* (Hooded Crane, *Grus monacha*) and the red-faced *manazuru* (White-naped Crane, *Grus vipio*)—wintered in Japan in great numbers, the latter giving their name to picturesque Cape Manazuru which juts out into Sagami Bay just southeast of Mt. Fuji.

The Common or European Crane (*Grus grus*) came sometimes too, as did the smaller Demoiselle Crane (*Anthropoides virgo*), the Siberian White Crane, and *Grus canadensis*. They appear rarely even now.

There are still two spots in southern Japan—Izumi in Kyushu and Yashiro, west of Iwakuni—where Hooded and White-naped Cranes fly in from across the Japan Sea to spend the winter; and watching them leave in February is a local event, these remnants of that varied host of cranes that once filled the marshlands and fields with its wingbeats and sonorous cries.

During the two and a half centuries of the Tokugawa shogunate (1603–1867), the migrant Hooded and White-naped Cranes were hunted, though in principle only by the shogun and his feudal lords, using mainly falcons for their sport. But the red-crested crane, long considered sacred, was inviolate in much of the main island and Kyushu. Officially, only one, at New Year, was allowed to be killed each year so that the emperor—himself divine—might partake of "broth of crane," a sacred elixir.

A thousand years before the Tokugawas, the adoption of Buddhism, instilling a respect for all forms of life, had introduced a relatively benign though impermanent influence on the treatment of the nation's wildlife, for hunting and eating meat were discouraged, and religious merit could be gained by releasing caged birds and other captive animals and pets. Indeed, the fifteenth day of the Eighth Moon (which falls in mid- or late September) was a sort of "Freeing Animals Day." The shrine of Iwashimizu-Hachiman on the outskirts of Kyoto still holds this rite every September 15 and has a pond into which fish are released.

73. Pair leaving a river (January).

One of Japan's first shoguns, Yoriyoshi of the Minamoto clan, built another shrine to Hachiman, the god of war, at Kamakura in 1063 in thanksgiving for his successful campaign against a rebellious northern clan. And his son Yoshiiye, who participated in the war, reportedly conducted in Kamakura a bird-freeing ceremony (*Hōjō-e*) that has been preserved for posterity in literature and art.

Seated by the original Hachiman Shrine's great gate near the sea, the general is depicted presiding over the release of numerous cranes, each with a gold or silver prayer-strip tied to its leg for the repose of the souls of those killed in the war. Moreover, Yoshiiye is said to have decreed that anyone capturing or killing a Japanese Crane thereafter would suffer the death penalty.

But, alas, when the period of the Tokugawa shoguns ended in 1868 and the new imperial government of Meiji was established, firearms were available for hunting, and no new law had been made to protect the Japanese Crane. The enormous birds were an easy target, and availing himself of his new freedom, the common man was eager to taste the broth once reserved for the emperor on New Year's Day and the meat that only the shogun and feudal lords had been allowed to eat.

In the brief span of twenty-five years or less, Japanese Cranes were all but wiped out in Japan, and until 1924, when a government official in Hokkaido heard that a hunter had seen some in the marshes near Kushiro, it was feared that the resident population of *Grus japonensis* had become extinct. Six nests were located by ornithologists, who estimated that there were probably about twenty birds altogether.

Although the shogun's edict against killing cranes had never been enforced in Hokkaido—Japan's northern island was too remote an outpost to matter—cranes had always been prolific there. But the Matsumae Chronicle of 1781 does record a distressing bag of three hundred cranes taken by hunters, and a 1784 document notes the export of salted cranes—this only from a tiny portion of Hokkaido, the single Japanese fief at its southernmost tip. Inhabited almost entirely by the crane-revering Ainu for centuries, the island was only settled in earnest by the Japanese at the turn of the century.

When the settlers arrived, they began by converting marshes into rice paddies, posing a more serious threat to the cranes by destroying their breeding grounds. Cranes thus disappeared from southwest and central Hokkaido.

In 1925, in the nick of time, 1,200 hectares (about 3,000 acres) of Kushiro Marsh were declared a protected area, and hunting was prohibited there. By 1930, the population of cranes had increased to about thirty. In 1935, more acreage was added and the Japanese Crane was declared a protected species.

Four years after the war, ornithologists were delighted to find the cranes still there, although their numbers were about the same. But it was not until artificial feeding was begun in 1952 that the crane population dramatically increased, though there are some who argue that cranes holding out in more isolated places may simply have discovered the feeding stations.

In 1967, the crane sanctuary was increased to a little over 5,000 hectares (about 12,500 acres), fifteen years after the bird itself was promoted to a higher category—that of *Tokubetsu Tennen Kinenbutsu*, Special Natural Treasure—giving it greater legal protection.

Tsuru Koen, a natural park for the Japanese Crane, was originally planned in 1935 by the Kushiro Crane Preservation Society, but only established in 1958. Covering an area of sixty-two hectares, it is unique—the only man-made breeding and feeding habitat for these birds. The land is low-lying peat, and a stream runs through it, from which an artificial marsh has been developed, planted with dropwort, reeds, and sedge, and stocked with loaches. There is also a woodland area with copses of silver birch, and one section has been planted with corn and buckwheat. A nine-foot wire-mesh fence encloses the park to keep out foxes and weasels.

Seven captured cranes were introduced into the park. Some breeding took place, as hoped, but problems arose with the natural incubation of eggs. Chicks, however, have been hatched and reared there artificially with great success, and the park now has eighteen tenants. Visible all the year round, unlike its wilder counterpart, the park's population provides an unusually intimate contact without the displacement and incarceration of a conventional zoo. The cranes have in fact become quite tame, and their playful ways have endeared their species to numerous visitors and done much to arouse nationwide interest in their future.

But the situation is far from satisfactory. The protected natural habitat is too small and unstable, as the following chapter will underline. Hazards to the crane proliferate. As many as eighteen cranes a year have been killed by colliding with electric power lines. These are hard for them to see when taking flight in alarm or when caught in unexpected wind currents. (In 1971 an attempt was made to make some of the cables more visible by hanging colored discs from them.)

The presence of lead shot in creeks and rivers, left there after the duck-shooting season, is also a threat, since cranes need pebbles for digestion and the little lead balls are poisonous.

Faced with these problems, ornithologists both in Japan and abroad are alarmed at the possibility that this wonderful creature may again be reduced in numbers, just when its future was looking a little brighter.

SAVE THE JAPANESE CRANE!

The requirements of Japanese Cranes are great and multifarious. Their reproductive potential is small—there are years when neither egg hatches—and they cannot reproduce at all if their individual territories are not sufficiently large. One breeding pair of birds in the wild needs an exclusive habitat of two square kilometers as a bare minimum, and preferably four to seven kilometers. They need the security of wet, inaccessible marshland for spring nesting, with plenty of reeds and other suitable material for nest-building. Less watery land for rearing the chicks when hatched should also be close at hand. Food must be abundantly available all spring and summer long. Fish, insects, molluscs, frogs and suchlike are hard to catch, and cranes—which prefer live animal food to plants—must search far and wide to obtain enough for their family needs. Lakes, ponds, rivers, and marsh shallows are all essential hunting areas because these are the habitats of the creatures cranes eat. Suitable summer roosting sites are needed too, not far from water and with clusters of shrubs. Rivers that do not freeze even in sub-zero temperatures are, of course, a prerequisite for winter roosting and food-seeking.

Such rivers are not abundant in eastern Hokkaido, but in the wake of urban and agricultural development, Hokkaido's southeast—Kushiro Marsh and a few smaller wetlands—has of necessity become the last bastion of the crane in Japan. We do not know what of the Asian population is left. Soviet scientists report the existence of only a score or two specimens still breeding in Siberia's Maritime Territory, now increasingly subject to reclamation, cultivation, and settlement. Before the Korean

War, hundreds and even thousands of birds migrated south every winter as far as the outskirts of Seoul.

Only a fraction of the bird's breeding grounds in Hokkaido is now protected. Unfortunately, even this portion is neither equipped with all the diverse elements needed for a balanced habitat, nor is it itself free from the danger of serious impairment as the development of peripheral areas continues. Marshes drastically change their character when surrounding woodlands are destroyed, and this is now happening. To feed its hungry mills, the paper industry is clearing the larches and alder trees from hill to hill in and around Kushiro Marsh, affecting the water table, which causes flooding and disrupts the chain of plant and animal life. More and more roads are being built and rivers embanked. Over half the southern portion of Kushiro Marsh has already been drained for farming, housing, or industry, making the remaining marsh too wet and causing the collapse of many of the hummocks where cranes have built their nests. In fact, we are facing a repetition of what happened to the marshes of the Ishikari Plain surrounding Hokkaido's capital, Sapporo, at the beginning of this century—with one major difference: speed. Bulldozers can demolish an entire hill in no time and turn verdant marshes into arid wastes in a matter of days.

Kushiro's marshlands were formed when the waters of Kushiro Bay receded thousands of years ago. But the coastal section of the marsh has long since disappeared.

Kushiro is a fast-growing port city with suburbs relentlessly swallowing up the surrounding greenery, and many of the hills bordering the marshes are bare but for the sturdy *sasa*, a bamboo grass pleasing to the eye but inhospitable to cranes.

Unless drastic measures are taken to place enough land under strict control for an adequate habitat with all the essential ecological qualities needed at least to sustain the present population of *Grus japonensis* in Hokkaido, the bird in the wild is doomed.

"Be a foster parent to a family of cranes!" and "Buy them a bit of marshland" are the slogans of an appeal soon to be launched in Japan under the auspices of the Wisconsin-based International Crane Foundation. Money from individuals and organizations will be collected to buy marshland for the cranes, so preserving a little more wilderness from the ravenous bulldozer. But the words on the title page of a report presented to the Japanese Government in 1972 by a concerned American ornithologist are still disturbingly pertinent: "We must act today or the majestic Japanese Crane will die out in Japan and perhaps the world." The Japanese Crested Ibis is almost extinct. It will be an even sadder day for everyone when the voice of *Grus japonensis* is silent, and fading images are all we have to remember its special beauty by.

74. Back at sundown to roost.

CRANE SPECIES

European Crane
Grus grus

Black-necked Crane
Grus nigricollis

Hooded Crane
Grus monacha

Sandhill Crane
Grus canadensis

Japanese Crane
Grus japonensis

American
Whooping Crane
Grus americana

White-naped Crane
Grus vipio

Sarus Crane
Grus antigone

Australian Crane
Grus rubicunda

Siberian
White Crane
Grus leucogeranus

Wattled Crane
Bugeranus carunculatus

Demoiselle Crane
Anthropoides virgo

Blue Crane
Anthropoides paradisea

Crowned Crane
Balearica pavonina
(regulorum)

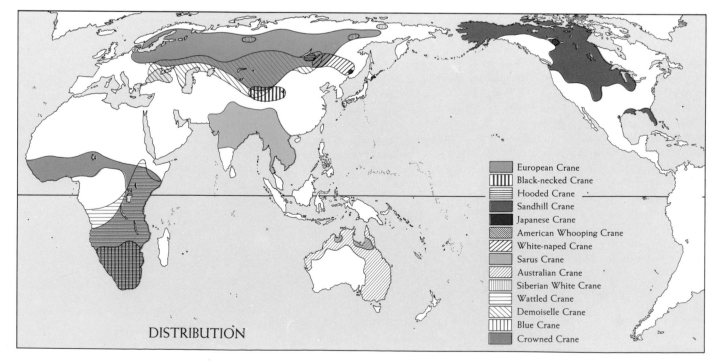

DISTRIBUTION

European Crane
Black-necked Crane
Hooded Crane
Sandhill Crane
Japanese Crane
American Whooping Crane
White-naped Crane
Sarus Crane
Australian Crane
Siberian White Crane
Wattled Crane
Demoiselle Crane
Blue Crane
Crowned Crane

BIBLIOGRAPHY

Archibald, George. "Conservation Report on *Grus japonensis.*" Presented to the Government of Japan. July, 1972.

Dementief, G. P., and Gladkov, N. A. *Birds of the Soviet Union.* Vol. 2. Israel Program for Scientific Translations. Jerusalem, 1969.

Hartland, Edwin Sidney. *The Science of Fairy Tales: An Inquiry into Fairy Mythology.* London: Methuen, 1925.

Hayashida, Tsuneo. *Tancho no Shiki.* Kagaku no Arubamu, no. 21. Tokyo: Akane Shobo, 1979.

——*Tancho: Konsen Genya ni Ikiru.* Tokyo: Heibonsha, 1976.

Keith, G. Stuart. "Rituals of Courtship Are Observed: The Last Colony of Japanese Cranes," in *Natural History,* 1962.

Koga, Tadamichi. "On the Cranes of Japan in the Wild and in Captivity," in *Zoologischer Garten N. F.* Jena, 1975.

Masatomi, Hiroyuki. *Tancho.* Hokkaido no Shizen, no. 6. Sapporo: Hokkaido Shinbunsha, 1977.

——and Kitagawa, Tamaki. "Bionomics and Sociology of Tancho or the Japanese Crane, *Grus japonensis.* I, Distribution, Habitat and Outline of Annual Cycle. II, Ethogram," in *The Journal of the Faculty of Science, Hokkaido University.* Vol. 19, nos. 3 and 4. Sapporo, 1974, 1975.

Takahashi, Ken. *Shitsugen ni Ikiru Tancho.* Tokyo: Kodansha, 1979.

"Tsuru," in *Anima,* no. 1. Tokyo: Heibonsha, 1975.

Walkinshaw, Lawrence. *Cranes of the World.* New York: Winchester Press, 1973.

Yamashina, Yoshimaro. *Birds in Japan.* Tokyo: Tokyo News Service, 1961.

INDEX (The plate numbers are in italics)

75. Sun sets over Kushiro Marsh and a solitary pair of cranes (April).

定価3,200円
in Japan